SANSKRIT HISTORICAL PHONOLOGY

A SIMPLIFIED OUTLINE FOR THE USE OF BEGINNERS IN SANSKRIT

BY
FRANKLIN EDGERTON

Sterling Professor of Sanskrit and Comparative Philology
In Yale Univeristy

WIPF & STOCK · Eugene, Oregon

Wipf and Stock Publishers
199 W 8th Ave, Suite 3
Eugene, OR 97401

Sanskrit Historical Phonology
A Simplified Outline for the Use of Beginners in Sanskrit
By Edgerton, Franklin and Harris, Zellig S.
Softcover ISBN-13: 978-1-7252-8105-9
Hardcover ISBN-13: 978-1-7252-8106-6
eBook ISBN-13: 978-1-7252-8107-3
Publication date 5/20/2020
Previously published by American Oriental Society,

SANSKRIT HISTORICAL PHONOLOGY

Franklin Edgerton
Yale University

Introductory note

For many years the present writer, like some of his colleagues, in teaching Sanskrit to beginners, has tried to introduce them not only to the language, but in some measure to its history, or better prehistory. This has involved the attempt to provide a rudimentary but systematic account of Indo-European phonology in relation to Sanskrit. The account must be very simple, or the average beginner, who usually has little knowledge of either Indo-European or the comparative method, will find it hard to assimilate.

No previously printed work appears to contain a statement satisfactory for this purpose. The closest approach is Thumb's *Handbuch*; excellent as it is in many ways, it is not what seems to me required.

What follows is nothing more than an attempt to satisfy this want. It is intended to furnish, in as simple a form as possible, the barest essentials of the subject: just what it seems to me a beginner must have, in order to get a sound view of the basic system, and no more. Profundity is eschewed. Controversial matters are avoided as far as possible. There is no pretension to either completeness or originality. Most of what is said is commonplace to all Indo-Europeanists. Only in matters connected with the semivowels have I felt compelled to go beyond the standard handbooks, for reasons made clear in certain recent publications, the chief of which is cited in § 60 below.

The regular development of each Indo-European sound in Sanskrit is illustrated by (usually) a single etymological correspondence. At the end a table of Sanskrit vowels, with their possible regular Indo-European correspondences, is provided. It has seemed unnecessary to do the like with the consonants.

My transliteration of Sanskrit follows that of Whitney and Lanman, the books commonly used by beginners in this country. I should have liked to use ś instead of ç, and to omit the macron over āi and āu, in accord with general usage today, but after some hesitation have decided against it. After even more hesitation, I have decided not to print accents on Sanskrit words, except when they particularly concern the subject under discussion. My reason is purely pedagogic. In the first year of Sanskrit, at least as commonly taught in this country, the student encounters no accented texts. He sees accents printed only in grammars and vocabularies or dictionaries. Is it profitable, or wise, to try to burden him at this stage with the pitch accents, which have no practical value in helping him to pronounce the words (indeed quite the reverse)?

My thanks are due to a number of colleagues who have offered helpful criticisms; especially to Professor George S. Lane of the University of North Carolina.

Outline of Sanskrit Historical Phonology

1. Sanskrit (abbreviated Skt.) in the following is always used in a wide sense to include the Vedic dialects. See the Introduction to Whitney's Grammar.

2. Indo-European (abbreviated IE) is the hypothetical prehistoric language from which Sanskrit as well as many other languages of Asia and most languages of Europe are demonstrably derived. To distinguish it from its descendants, it is also often called Proto-Indo-European or Primitive Indo-European (abbreviated PIE).

3. The Indo-European languages (the historic descendants of this prehistoric language) are often divided into two groups, called the satem and the centum languages. This division is based on their several treatments of the IE guttural consonants; see § 21. The division is traditional, and is sometimes convenient, but it suggests more than the proved facts justify. The two groups are distinguished by nothing else than their treatment of the gutturals. The classification should not be taken as meaning that each group is descended from an original distinct language more recent than Proto-Indo-European.

4. The satem languages are in general the eastern division of the family, geographically speaking. The principal satem languages are Indo-Iranian (including Sanskrit and other Indic languages on the one hand, and the Iranian languages, of which the two oldest are Avestan and Old Persian, on the other), Armenian, Albanian, and Balto-Slavic.

5. The centum languages are in general the western group. Their principal representatives are Greek, Italic (including Oscan-Umbrian as well as Latin), Germanic, and Celtic.

6. Illustrative examples in this outline will mostly be taken from Sanskrit, Greek, Latin, and Germanic languages. The latter include Gothic (Gth.), Old Norse (ON.), Old English (OE.), Old Saxon (OS.), Old High German (OHG.), and Old Frisian, besides later dialects. Occasionally cognates will be quoted from Avestan (Av.), Lithuanian (Lith.; a Baltic language), Old Slavic (and Russian), and Old Irish (OIr.); very rarely from others.

7. The phonemic system of IE contained *vowels, semivowels,* and *consonants.*

Consonants

8. The IE consonant system consisted almost wholly of *stops.* The following table shows the stops attributed to IE.

Labials	p	ph	b	bh
Dentals	t	th	d	dh
Palatals	k̂	k̂h	ĝ	ĝh
Velars	k	kh	g	gh
Labiovelars	k^w	k^wh	g^w	g^wh

The palatals, velars, and labiovelars are called collectively gutturals.

9. The *voiceless aspirates* ph, th, etc. are indistinguishable from the voiceless non-aspirates in all other languages than Indo-Iranian, except that Greek has aspirates for some of them (not all). Even in Sanskrit they are not very common, and not all of them can be illustrated by convincing etymologies in the other languages. The exponents of the Indo-Hittite laryngeal hypothesis derive them from pre-IE stops followed by laryngeals: Sturtevant, *Laryngeals,* § 78; cf. below, § 138. We shall ignore the voiceless aspirates for the most part.

10. *Germanic* correspondences can be understood only in terms of Grimm's Law and Verner's Law. By *Grimm's Law*—

	[1] IE	p, t, k	become	Proto-Germanic	f, þ, h (ch)
and	[1] IE	ph, th, kh	"	"	f, þ, h (ch)
	IE	b, d, g	"	"	p, t, k
	IE	bh, dh, gh	"	"	b, d, g

The Proto-Germanic sounds written b, d, g may have been voiced spirants rather than stops.

11. In High German, some further shifts took place; thus, general Germanic p, t, k (from IE b, d, g) became either f (ff), s (ss), ch, or pf, ts, kh (k plus ch). These High German changes we shall not describe in detail.

12. By *Verner's Law,* Proto-Germanic f, þ, h (from IE p, t, k, or ph, th, kh) became voiced when the preceding syllable was not

---

[1] However, after Proto-Germanic spirants (s, from IE s, and f, þ, h) these sounds appear as Germanic p, t, k.

accented in IE. They then coincided with Proto-Germanic b, d, g (whether these were spirants or stops). Verner's Law also involves IE and Proto-Germanic s, which changed to z when the preceding syllable was not accented in IE. In North and West Germanic (= all Germanic except Gothic) this z became r.

13. *The law of two aspirates, or Grassmann's Law.* In Sanskrit and in Greek (independently of each other), an aspirate at the beginning of a syllable loses its aspiration if another aspirate comes at the end of the same syllable or at the beginning of the next. In Greek this change took place after the voiced aspirates had become voiceless φ, θ, χ; consequently the deaspirated stops are always voiceless π, τ, κ (not voiced β, δ, γ). Ex.: IE stem dhrugh- 'injurious'; Skt. gen. sg. druh-as, but nom. sg. dhruk (because in the nom. the aspiration of the final is lost). Cf. Gk. τριχός, gen. sg. 'of the hair,' but nom. sg. θρίξ (IE dhrigh-).

14. IE p = Skt. p

IE septm̥ 'seven': Skt. sapta; Gk. ἑπτά; Lat. septem; Gth. OHG. sibun, OE. seofon, Eng. seven (problematic as to loss of t, and as to n for m); OSlav. sedmь (Russ. sjemj),[2] also problematic.

15. IE b = Skt. b (a strangely rare sound in IE)

IE root bel, bol 'strong': Skt. bala- 'strength,' baliṣṭha- 'strongest'; Gk. βελτίων, βέλτερος 'stronger'; perhaps Lat. dē-bilis 'lacking in strength, weak'; OSlav. boljьjь[2] 'greater,' Russ. bóljeye adv., 'more,' boljshóy 'great.'

16. IE bh = Skt. bh

IE bhū (zero grade to bhewə) 'become, come to be, be': Skt. aorist 3 sg. a-bhū-t 'became'; Gk. ἔ-φῡ; OLat. fū-ī (later fuī); ON. OE. OHG. bū (noun) 'dwelling,' OE. plur. by (from a form with suffix containing i), Ger. Bau; Lith. búti, infin., 'to be'; OSlav. byti, Russ. bytj 'to be.'

17. IE t = Skt. t

IE stem tri-, nom. pl. masc. treyes 'three': Skt. tri-, trayas; Gk. τρι-, τρεῖς (dial. τρέες, for treyes); Lat. trēs; Gth. þreis, Eng. three; OSlav. trьje, trije, nt. tri; Russ. trji.

---

[2] In Russian we represent a palatalized consonant by consonant plus j. In OSlav. (Old Bulgarian, Church Slavic), ъ represents a reduced vowel of u quality, and ь one of i quality.

18. IE th = Skt. th

In 2 sg. perfect ending IE -tha: Skt. -tha; Gk. -θα; Gth. -t; e. g. Skt. vet-tha 'thou knowest'; Gk. οἶσ-θα; Gth. wais-t, Ger. weisst.

19. IE d = Skt. d

IE dek̑m̥ 'ten': Skt. daça; Gk. δέκα; Lat. decem; Gth. taihun (with n for m, somewhat problematic), Eng. ten; Lith. dẽšimt(s); OSlav. desętь (Russ. djésjatj) 'ten' (the Balto-Slavic words originally collectives, 'a decad,' with IE suffix -ti-).

20. IE dh = Skt. dh

IE dhūmo- 'smoke, steam, mist': Skt. dhūma- 'smoke, mist'; Gk. θυμός 'spirit, excitement, passion'; Lat. fūmus 'smoke'; Lith. dúmai, pl., 'smoke'; OSlav. dymъ, Russ. dym, 'smoke.'

21. *The three series of gutturals.* As was said above, the IE languages fall into two groups as regards their treatment of these consonants.

I. In the eastern group—Indo-Iranian, Armenian, Albanian, and Balto-Slavic—the *velars* and *labiovelars* fall together, appearing as plain velars (that is, the labiovelars lose the labialization); while the *palatals* in general become *sibilants.*

II. In the western group—Greek, Italic, Celtic, and Germanic—the palatals and velars fall together, while the labiovelars remain distinct.

Group I is called the *satem* languages (Avestan satəm '100'), Group II the *centum* languages (Lat. centum).

22. *The Indo-European palatals.* In most of the satem languages these, as we saw, appear as sibilants. This is the case in Skt. as regards the voiceless k̑.

23. IE k̑ = Skt. ç

IE k̑m̥tom '100': Skt. çatam; Avestan satəm; Gk. (ἑ-)κατόν; Lat. centum; OIrish cét, Welsh cant; Gth. hund; Lith. šim̃tas; OSlav. sъtó, Russ. sto (for vocalism, see § 103).

24. But the IE voiced palatals (non-aspirate and aspirate) do *not* become sibilants, before and after vowels, in Sanskrit. (In certain phonetic conditions they do, or once did; see §§ 39, 40.) Sanskrit is unique among all the satem languages in this respect, and strangely destroys the parallelism otherwise existing between voiced and voiceless consonants.

25. IE ĝ = Skt. j

IE root ĝenə, ĝonə, zero grade ĝn̥̄ 'beget'; numerous derivatives in most IE languages. Thus, IE ĝenos- (nt.) : Skt. janas- 'tribe, people'; Gk. γένος 'birth, race' etc.; Lat. genus. Slightly different suffix in Avestan zana- 'people' (note Iranian sibilant). See § 152 for ĝn̥̄-to-. The root is lost, or nearly so, in Balto-Slavic.

26. IE ĝh = Skt. h

IE root ĝhey, zero grade ĝhi 'cold, snow'; generally with m-affixes (or is m part of the original root? not wholly clear). Normal grade: Skt. heman- 'winter'; Gk. χεῖμα, χειμών 'winter'; Lith. žiemà; OSlav. zima, Russ. zjimá 'winter.' (Note sibilants in Balto-Slavic.) Zero grade: Skt. hima- 'snow,' himā 'winter'; Gk. (δύσ-)χιμος 'wintry'; Lat. bīmus for bi-himus 'two winters (i. e. years) old.'

Related but problematic are Gk. χιών 'snow'; Lat. hiems 'winter'; Avestan zaēn- 'winter' (note Iranian sibilant).

27. The IE *velars* and *labiovelars* fall together in Skt. as in the other satem languages. But tho their development is identical, it is two-fold. (Slavic has a similar double treatment of them.)

In general, they both appear as plain velars (or gutturals): Skt. k, g, gh.

But when followed by an Indo-European front vowel or semivowel—that is, before IE e, ē, i, ī, y (which appear in Skt. as a, ā, i, ī, y)—they are changed to Sanskrit palatals: Skt. c, j, h.[3] (But before Skt. a, ā when these represent IE a, o, ā, ō, Skt. regularly has gutturals.)

Note that *these Sanskrit* 'palatals' are, then, not derived from IE 'palatals' (k̂, ĝ, ĝh), but from IE k or k^w, g or g^w, gh or g^wh.

Confusing, however, is the fact that, as we just saw, the IE *voiced* palatals (ĝ, ĝh), between vowels at least, *do* appear as Skt. palatal j, and as h, respectively: the same sounds which, before IE front vowels and semivowels, also represent IE voiced velars and labiovelars.

In other words, Skt. j and h are, in themselves, ambiguous as to

---

[3] Structurally and historically, Skt. h may be classed as a 'palatal'; see § 45.

origin. Not so Skt. c, which can only come from a velar or labiovelar (k or k^w); for IE palatal k̂ gives Skt. ç, a sibilant.

28. IE k = Skt. k or c

IE krewəs-: Skt. kraviṣ- 'meat, raw flesh'; Gk. κρέ(ϝ)ας 'meat.' Related: (o-grade, different suffixes) Lith. kraũjas 'blood'; OE. hrēaw, Eng. raw; (zero-grade IE krū-, before vowels kruw-) Skt. krū-ra- 'bloody, cruel'; Lat. cruor (IE *kruwōs) 'blood'; OSlav. krъvь, Russ. krovj 'blood' (IE *kruwi-).

In this group of words there is no opportunity for the double representation, which may be illustrated by the two closely related and almost synonymous adjectives Skt. çukra- 'bright' and çuci- 'shining, clear,' both from a root Skt. çuc or çuk 'shine.'

29. IE g = Skt. g or j

IE awg- 'be strong,' awges- 'strength': Skt. ojas- 'strength'; related are Lat. augus-tus 'mighty, exalted,' Lat. augeō; Gth. aukan, OE. ēacian 'increase,' Eng. eke (verb and adverb). But, from zero grade IE ug-, before a consonant, Skt. ug-ra- 'strong, fierce.'

30. IE gh = Skt. gh or h

IE root dhrewgh (dhrowgh), zero grade dhrugh 'injure, deceive': Skt. druh-yati 'injures' (d for dh by Grassmann's Law, § 13; h before y), Vedic drogha- (IE dhrowgho-) 'injury'; OSaxon driogan, OHG. triogan, Ger. be-trügen.

31. IE k^w = Skt. k or c

Note: in Greek, the labiovelars (but not the plain velars) have double representation, determined by the following sound, like the velars and labiovelars in Sanskrit. Before e and i vowels they appear as dentals, τ, δ, θ; otherwise as labials, π, β, φ.

IE k^wo-, k^wi-, interrogative pronoun: Skt. ka- 'who?', cid (orig. 'what?', used only as adverbial particle; kim 'what?' is analogical both in initial k- and in ending -m); Gk. πό-θεν 'whence?', τί-ς 'who?'; Lat. quo-, qui-; Gth. hwas 'who?', OE. hwā, Eng. who; and OE. hwī, hwiu 'how, why?', Eng. why; Lith. kàs 'who?'; OSlav. kъ-to (Russ. kto) 'who?', gen. česo 'whose?'

32. IE g^w = Skt. g or j

(Cf. § 31, Note.) IE g^wōw- 'cow, ox': Skt. gāu-; Gk. βοῦς; Lat. bōs (Oscan-Umbrian loanword; regular Latin would have initial v-); OE cū, Eng. cow; OSlav. gov-ędo, cf. Russ. govjádjina 'beef.'

IE g^wīwo- 'alive': Skt. jīva- 'alive'; Lat. vīvus; Lith. gývas; OSlav. zhivъ, Russ. zhiv 'alive.' Regular Greek δ perhaps in δίαιτα 'manner of life.' (In Greek βίος 'life,' cf. § 147, β is problematic.)

33. IE g^wh = Skt. gh or h

(Cf. § 31, Note.) IE root g^when, g^whon, g^whn̥ 'smite, slay': Skt. hanti (IE g^when-ti) 'he slays,' noun ghana- 'slaying' (both adj. and noun; IE g^whono-); Gk. θείνω 'I slay' (IE g^whenyō), φόνος 'murder' (= Skt. ghana-); OHG. gund-fano 'war-banner'; Lith. genù, 1 sg. pres., giñti infin., 'drive (with blows)'; OSlav. gъnati, Russ. gnatj, 'drive, hunt,' and general Slav. noun gonъ, gon 'pursuit' etc. (= Skt. ghana-, Gk. φόνος; Russ. in compounds and derivatives, e. g. gonjítj 'drive').

34. *Sibilants.* The only absolutely certain IE sibilant phoneme was

IE s = Skt. s

IE septm̥ 'seven': Skt. sapta; Gk. ἑπτά, etc., see § 14.

35. It is pretty certain that this s automatically became voiced z in IE in certain phonetic situations; in other situations it may have been otherwise modified. Some believe that IE had a phonemically distinct z, at least; this seems to me doubtful.

36. *IE þ, and voiced correspondents.* Only after guttural consonants (k̂, k, k^w etc.), IE seems in some words to show a set of mysterious consonants which appear as dentals (t etc.) in Greek and Celtic, but as s or sh sounds in Indo-Iranian, Italic, Germanic and Balto-Slavic. It is customary to assume that these consonants were similar to the voiceless English *th* in *thin,* and its voiced counterpart in *this.* The sounds are written þ, đ, đh. It seems to me doubtful whether our current theories have got at the truth on this point. A simple instance of the voiceless sound:

IE þ (?) = Skt. ṣ

IE r̥k̂þo- 'bear' (the animal): Skt. r̥kṣa-; Gk. ἄρκτος; Lat. ursus; Middle Irish art 'bear.'

37. *Sanskrit 'linguals' or domals or cerebrals.* Sanskrit has a series of sounds, transliterated ṭ, ṭh, ḍ, ḍh, ṇ, ṣ, called by the above (or still different) names, which have no correspondents in any other Indo-European language. So far as they are of IE origin at all, these domals mostly are modifications of IE dentals.

38. The dental nasal n regularly becomes domal ṇ under the conditions stated in Whitney 189; the dental sibilant s becomes domal ṣ by Whitney 180; a dental immediately following a domal in the same word is mostly domalized (details in Whitney 196 ff.).

39. Further, by regular phonetic development, IE palatals under certain conditions (notably before IE dentals and in final position) become domals; and a following dental is then also made domal. See Whitney 218, 219, 222; Wackernagel I §§ 120, 149.

IE root dik̂-: Skt. diçati 'shows,' but participle diṣṭa- 'shown.'

IE root yeĝ-, zero grade iĝ-, 'revere': Skt. yajati 'worships,' but pple. iṣṭa-. (Contrast IE root yug-, with velar g: Skt. yug-a(m) 'yoke' and yuj- 'joining' (chiefly in cpds.), pple. yukta-.)

40. The IE palatal voiced aspirate ĝh combined with following dental, most commonly t, in prehistoric Indo-Iranian, forming the cluster *ždh, for theoretical IE ĝh-t which became (perhaps in IE itself) ĝdh (just so in Skt. we regularly find theoretical gh-t, dh-t, bh-t becoming respectively gdh, ddh, bdh; Whitney 160). This *ždh in Skt. lost the voiced sibilant, which however left its trace in domalization of dh to ḍh, and lengthening of a preceding short vowel:

IE root leyĝh, liĝh 'lick': Skt. lihati 'licks,' but participle līḍha- 'licked.' Here a theoretical IE *liĝh-to- became first, perhaps in IE itself, liĝ-dho-, which became Indo-Iranian liždha-, Skt. līḍha-.

41. Aside from the cases of §§ 38-40, the Sanskrit domals do not occur in genuinely native Sanskrit words.

42. The words containing them are partly non-Aryan, partly of Middle Indic origin; in either case, borrowed from dialects other than that on which Sanskrit is primarily based.

43. In many Middle Indic dialects, Sanskrit dentals have become domals: in some cases universally, in others in certain phonetic surroundings, especially when a Skt. consonantal or vocalic r (which has domal articulation in Skt.) adjoined the dental. Many such words were borrowed from these Middle Indic dialects into Sanskrit itself.

44. Thus the Sanskrit word kṛta- 'made' became in many MI dialects kaṭa-; the change of ṛ to a is also MIndic; domal ṭ is due to the original ṛ. This kaṭa-, in certain compounds, was borrowed into Skt., e. g. Skt. vikaṭa- 'distorted, ugly.' But the genuine Skt. vikṛta- likewise exists, meaning 'modified, altered,' but also 'malformed, disfigured, maimed' and the like. This and many similar cases prove that the domals, in words of this type, are really foreign to original Sanskrit; even if of Indo-European origin, they are the result of Middle Indic sound changes, and appear in Skt. only by borrowing.

45. *Sanskrit h.* This sound, a 'murmured' h or voiced glottal spirant, is classed by the Hindus as phonetically a guttural. Historically, we have already seen that it is the regular representative of IE ĝh, the palatal voiced aspirate, under all circumstances, and of IE gh, g^wh, the velar and labiovelar voiced aspirates, before IE front vowels and semivowels. Structurally it may be regarded as the aspirate corresponding to Skt. j (palatal).

46. But also, h not infrequently replaces dh. So to root dhā 'place,' the past passive participle is hita- (for dhita-). In a very few cases, also, it represents bh: the root grabh 'seize' also appears as grah. The conditions under which h replaced dh and bh are obscure, but doubtless dialectal (i. e. due to dialect loans, as in the case of many domals). It is worth noting that many Middle Indic dialects replace most Skt. aspirate stops (primarily between vowels) by h.

47. *The Sanskrit palatal aspirates.* Skt. ch and jh are said by the Hindu phoneticians to stand in the same relation to c and j that the other aspirates do to the non-aspirates. But historically and structurally the case is otherwise.

48. jh exists only in loanwords (from either Middle Indic or non-Aryan dialects), and in a few sound-imitative words. It is, in other words, hardly a normal Skt. phoneme. Cf. § 45; the aspirate to j is h.

49. ch also occurs in some loanwords. When derived directly from IE, it is the resultant of a combination of IE s with k̑ or k̑h (possibly also k, kh). Consistent with this origin is the fact that ch is always a double or long consonant; even if a preceding vowel is short, the syllable is prosodically long, as always before more than one consonant. It is often written double, that is, preceded by c; but there can be no really meaningful distinction between ch and cch; some rules are given, but it is nothing but a matter of orthographic convention.

50. IE sk̑, sk̑h = Skt. ch

IE gʷm̥-sk̑eti 'goes': Skt. gachati (usually written gacchati); Gk. βάσκω.

IE root sk̑hid 'split': Skt. root chid- 'split'; Gk. σχίζω; Lat. scindō. (Some, on the basis of Baltic forms, assume IE skh- here.)

Vowels

51. There were three IE short vowels, a, e, o; and three long vowels, ā, ē, ō. Sanskrit has merged each set of three into a single vowel which we write a, ā. We have seen in § 27 that it nevertheless shows some traces of the original distinction, at any rate of that between e, ē on the one hand, and a, o, ā, ō on the other.

52. IE a = Skt. a

IE ag̑ro- 'field': Skt. ajra- 'field, plain'; Gk. ἀγρός; Lat. ager; Gth. akrs, Ger. Acker, Eng. acre.

53. IE ā = Skt. ā

IE bhrātor-, bhrāter-: Skt. bhrātar-; Gk. φρά̄τηρ 'tribesman'; Lat. frāter; Gth. brōþar, Eng. brother; Lith. broterė̃lis (dim.); OSlav. bratrъ, bratъ. (The latter may represent the IE nom. sg. bhrātē, bhrātō: Skt. bhrātā; but the relation of the two forms is disputed.)

54. IE e = Skt. a

IE esti '(he, she, it) is': Skt. asti; Gk. ἐστί; Lat. est; Ger. ist; (Old) Lith. esti; OSlav. (j)estь, Russ. (y)estj.

55. IE ē = Skt. ā

IE root dhē- 'put, place': Skt. dhā-, as in dadhāti 'puts, places,' dhāna- 'receptacle, place for setting (something)'; Gk. τί-θη-μι 'I place,' ἔ-θηκα 'I placed'; Lat. fēcī (originally) 'I placed,' and con-dō 'I put together'; OSaxon de-da, OHG. te-ta 'I did'; OSlav. děją, děti 'place,' Russ. djetj 'to put.'

IE sēmi (adv., and prefix) 'one-half'; Skt. sāmi (chiefly in compounds); Gk. ἡμι- (only in cpds.); Lat. sēmi; OHG. sāmi.

56. IE o = Skt. a

IE poti- ‘lord, husband’: Skt. pati- ‘lord, husband’; Gk. πόσις ‘husband’; Lat. *potis ‘able’ (possum for potis sum ‘I am able’); Gth. -faþs ‘lord’ (in brūþ-faþs ‘bride-lord, bridegroom,’ hunda-faþs ‘lord of a hundred, centurion’); Lith. patìs, pàts ‘husband.’

Fem. IE potnī- ‘lady, mistress, wife’: Skt. patnī; Gk. πότνια; OLith. -patni ‘mistress, female possessor.’

57. IE ō = Skt. ā

IE root dō ‘give’: Skt. da-dā-ti ‘gives,’ dāna- ‘gift’; Gk. δί-δω-μι ‘I give,’ δῶ-ρον ‘gift’; Lat. dō-num; Lith. dúo-ti ‘to give’; OSlav. da-ti, Russ. datj ‘to give,’ OSlav. darъ ‘gift,’ (antiquated) Russ. dar, cf. Russ. dárom ‘(as a gift,) for nothing, in vain.’

Semivowels

58. IE had six phonemes called semivowels, each of which could function as a vowel, as a consonant, or as a vowel plus a (homorganic) consonant. In these three forms they were:

Vocalic form	Consonantal form	Vocalic plus consonantal
i	y	iy
u	w	uw
r̥	r	r̥r
l̥	l	l̥l
m̥	m	m̥m
n̥	n	n̥n

59. We call each of these six units a *phoneme*, that is, a ‘minimum unit of distinctive sound-feature’ (L. Bloomfield, *Language* 79). It is characteristic of a phoneme that, while it may be pronounced differently under different conditions, these differences of pronunciation are automatically regulated by the surrounding features. The various phonetically differing forms of a phoneme are called its *positional variants* or *allophones*. Thus *i*, *y*, and *iy* are three allophones of a single phoneme. It doesn’t matter what sign we choose to represent a phoneme, but we might use /y/ for this one, and /w r l m n/ for the other five semivowels of IE. Slanting bars are used to enclose phonemes, in writing and print.

60. The conditions determining each positional variant of a semivowel in IE were first fully formulated (as far as they can now be determined) by the writer in *Language* 19.83 ff. (1943): 'The Indo-European Semivowels.' When more than one semivowel came together the results are rather complicated and in part obscure; see my summary p. 108 f. When one semivowel was preceded and followed by no other semivowel, but only by a vowel and/or a consonant, the fairly simple rules are stated pp. 84-87. Here is a still briefer summary:

I. A semivowel was vocalic (i, u, r̥, l̥, m̥, n̥) between consonants, or in sentence-initial or sentence-final position before or after a consonant.

II. It was consonantal (y, w, r, l, m, n):

(1) Between vowels, or in sentence-initial or sentence-final position before or after a vowel;

(2) After a vowel and before a consonant;

(3) After a consonant and before a vowel, provided the preceding consonant was itself preceded by a *short* vowel.

III. It was vocalic plus consonantal (iy, uw, r̥r, l̥l, m̥m, n̥n) after a consonant and before a vowel, if the preceding consonant was *not* preceded by a *short* vowel; that is, if it was preceded by another consonant, a *long* vowel, or nothing (in sentence initial).

61. Such was the condition of the semivowels in IE. It is best preserved in the Rigveda, but not perfectly even there. In most IE languages, we find only remnants or vestiges of it, in particular categories of forms. In Classical Sanskrit it is still preserved to a large extent, tho much less perfectly than in the Rigveda.

62. In Sanskrit, then, i and y and iy have come to be in part distinct phonemes; and so have the descendants of IE u and w and uw, r̥ and r and r̥r, etc.; that is, they are only in part automatic variants of each other under definable conditions.

63. Furthermore, historical changes have disguised the forms assumed by some of the positional variants of some of the IE semivowels.

64. Accordingly, it is necessary, for clarity, to treat these positional variants (at least in part) as separate and independent sounds as to their development in Sanskrit.

65. IE i = Skt. i

IE owi- 'sheep': Skt. avi-; Gk. ὄ(ϝ)ις; Lat. ovis; OIr. ōi; Gth. awi-str 'sheep-fold,' OE. ēowe, ēowu (Eng. ewe); Lith. avìs 'sheep'; OSlav. ovь-tsa, Russ. ovtsá 'sheep.'

66. IE y = Skt. y (except as in II (2), § 60).

IE yugo-(m) 'yoke': Skt. yuga-m; Gk. ζυγόν; Lat. jugum; Gth. juk, OE. geoc (Eng. yoke), Ger. Joch; OSlav. Russ. (antiquated) igo (from yugom > *jъgo > *jьgo by assimilation > igo) 'yoke.'

67. *But*: after a vowel and before a consonant (II (2), § 60) or at the end of an utterance, that is when forming what is called a *diphthong* (IE ay, ey, oy: āy, ēy, ōy), before a consonant or in sentence final, y has special treatment in Skt.; and it often has in other IE languages. The diphthongs containing y (and w) have a tendency, all over the IE field, to change to monophthongs; that is, vowel plus consonantal semivowel y or w (especially when followed by a consonant or final) often becomes some sort of simple vowel.

68. In Sanskrit, IE ay, ey, oy are all treated alike (since as we saw IE a, e, o all become a), and all become a monophthong e, when followed by a consonant or at the end of an utterance.

This e however is *always long.* (Sanskrit has no short e-vowel.)

69. IE ay = Skt. e

IE aydhos- 'fire; burning; firewood'; Skt. edhas- 'firewood'; Gk. αἶθος (nt.) 'fire.'

Also IE aydho-, same mg.: Skt. edha- 'firewood'; Gk. αἶθος (m.), 'fire'; cf. Lat. aed-ēs 'hearth; home'; OE. ād, OHG. eit 'funeral pyre.'

70. IE ey = Skt. e

IE root deyk̂- 'point out': Skt. di-deṣ-ṭi 'points,' deça- '(direction,) region'; Gk. δείκ-νυμι 'I show'; OLat. deico, Lat. dīcō 'I say' (orig. 'show'); Gth. ga-teih-an 'to indicate,' OE. tīon, OHG. zīhan (Ger. zeihen) 'to accuse' (OHG. zeigōn, Ger. zeigen, from IE doyk̂-, § 71, with g by Verner's law, § 12; probably denominative).

71. IE oy = Skt. e

IE woyda '(I have seen,) I know,' perfect to root weyd- 'see': Skt. veda 'I know'; Gk. (ϝ)οἶδα 'I know' (cf. εἶδον 'I saw');

Gth. wait, Eng. wot, Ger. weiss 'I know'; OPrussian (a Baltic language) waisse 'thou knowest.'

72. The long y diphthongs—combinations of IE ā, ē, ō with y—remain long diphthongs in Skt.; they are commonly transcribed āi (or ai).

73. IE āy = Skt. āi

In dat. sg. ending of fem. ā-stems, IE -āy: Skt. -āi (e.g. senāy-āi); Gk. -ᾳ (= -āy; e.g. χώρ-ᾳ); Lat. mēns-ae.

74. IE ēy = Skt. āi

In stem syllable of s-aorist of roots containing y: IE e-lēykʷ-sm̥(m) (before vowel -m̥m, before consonant -m̥) 'I left': Skt. arāikṣam; Gk. ἔλειψα (each generalizing one of the two alternants).

75. IE ōy = Skt. āi

In dat. sg. ending of o-stems, IE -ōy: Skt. (dev-)āy(-a) 'to a god'; Gk. (ἵππ-)ῳ; Praenestine (Italic) (Numasi-)oi (Lat. -ō); Lith. (vil̃k-)ui 'to a wolf.'

76. IE u, w, and uw behave in Skt. quite analogously to IE i, y, iy. Here w appears as a sound transcribed v (actually pronounced in some positions as w), u as u. The diphthongs aw, ew, ow appear as Skt. o (always long! like Skt. e); and āw, ēw, ōw, as (what we write as) āu (or au).

77. IE u = Skt. u

IE yugo- 'yoke,' etc., see § 66.

78. IE w = Skt. v

IE woyda 'I know,' etc., see § 71.

79. IE aw = Skt. o

IE root awg- 'increase, strengthen'; IE awges-, awgos- 'strength': Skt. ojas 'strength'; Lat. augus-tus 'mighty, exalted.' Cf. Lat. aug-eō 'I increase'; Gth. aukan, OE. ēacian 'to increase,' Eng. eke (verb and adverb).

80. IE ew = Skt. o

IE root lewk- and lowk- 'shine.' IE lewk-etay 'shines'; Skt. roc-ate 'shines.' Cf. Gk. λευκός 'shining, white'; Gth. liuhaþ 'light,' OE. lēoht, Eng. light.

81. IE ow = Skt. o

IE lowk-, see preceding. Forms from IE ow (rather than ew) are: IE (causative) lowkeyeti 'makes to shine': Skt. rocayati, same mg.; Lat. lūceō (originally transitive, in OLat. 'light (a lamp),' later intrans.); IE lowko- 'light space': Skt. loka- 'world'; OLat. loucom (acc.), Lat. lūcus 'clearing in a wood, grove,' cf. Lat. collūcāre 'to thin out (a forest)'; OE. lēah (Eng. lea), ON. lō, Dutch lō, loo (Water-loo), 'meadow' (= clear space).

82. IE āw = Skt. āu

IE nāw-, nom. nāws 'ship': Skt. nāu-(s); Gk. ναῦς (gen. νηός for *νᾱϝός); Lat. nāv-i-s (has become an i-stem); OIr. náu; ON. nōr, OE. nō-wend 'shipmaster, sailor.'

83. IE ew = Skt. āu

IE dyēw-(s, nom. sg.) 'sky, god of heaven': Skt. dyāu-(s); Gk. Ζεύς (for older *Ζηυς); (Lat. Jū-piter, Juppiter, from IE dyew, voc. used as nom.;) ON. Tȳr, OE. (Tīg,) gen. Tīwes (Eng. Tuesday, 'Tīg's day').

84. IE ōw = Skt. āu

IE g^wōw-(s, nom.) 'cow, ox'; Skt. gāu-(s); Gk. βοῦς (acc. dialectal βῶν); (Lat. bōs, loan from an Italic dialect, with vowel taken from acc. IE g^wōm;) OE. cū, Eng. cow.

85. The vocalic-consonantal forms of the phonemes /y w/, namely iy, uw, require no special treatment in Sanskrit; they appear as Skt. iy, uv, exactly as if i plus y, u plus w.

86. Coming to the four other semivowel phonemes, IE /r l m n/, their Sanskrit developments are in some ways simpler, in others more complicated than IE /y w/. The perfect parallelism between the six IE semivowels has partly broken down in Sanskrit.

87. As to the diphthongal forms, which required special treatment for /y w/, no such special treatment is needed for /r l m n/. After any IE vowel (a, e, o; ā, ē, ō), appearing in Skt. as a or ā, IE r, l, m, n are treated as any other r, l, m, n (after a consonant, or initially). We don't need, therefore, to state special rules for IE ar, er, or, etc., in Skt.

88. The chief complications concerning /r l m n/ are the following:

1. The phonemes /r/ and /l/, in vocalic and consonantal and

vocalic-plus-consonantal forms, both merged in one phoneme /r/ in prehistoric Indo-Iranian. They have that form in Old Iranian (Avestan and Old Persian). In Sanskrit, /l/ was introduced secondarily, for Indo-Iranian /r/ in some occurrences, still in prehistoric times. But since it always has passed through a stage when there was only /r/, Skt. /l/ shows no correlation with IE /l/; it just as often represents IE /r/. And Skt. /r/ represents IE /l/ as often as IE /r/.

2. The vocalic-consonantal allophones of IE /r l/, namely IE r̥r, l̥l, appear in Sanskrit as ir or ur (or, less commonly, as il, ul, because of the preceding law).

3. The vocalic allophones of /m, n/, namely IE m̥, n̥, appear in Skt. alike as a. And so, IE m̥m appears as Skt. am, IE n̥n as Skt. an. Greek has the same treatment, α for IE m̥, n̥.

89. IE r̥ = Skt. ṛ

IE r̥k̑þo-: Skt. ṛkṣa- 'bear' (the animal), etc., see § 36.

90. IE l̥ = Skt. ṛ

IE wl̥kʷo- 'wolf': Skt. vṛka-; Gth. wulfs, Eng. wolf; Lith. vil̃kas; OSlav. vlъkъ, Russ. volk 'wolf.' (The f of Germanic must have replaced an older hw; just how or why is disputed.)

Note: every provable IE l̥ in Skt. appears only as ṛ. In fact, Skt. ḷ is found only in forms of the single root kḷp- 'fashion, form,' e. g. kḷpta- 'formed'; nowhere else. The etymology of this root is doubtful; some think it related to Lat. corpus 'body'; if so, Skt. ḷ would be from IE r̥ in the single root which shows it.

91. IE r = Skt. r or l

IE root reudh-, roudh-, rudh- 'red.' The other languages than Indo-Iranian show only r: Gk. ἐ-ρεύθω 'redden,' ἐρυθρός 'red'; Lat. rūbidus, ruber, etc.; Gth. rauþs 'red,' OE. rēad, Eng. red; Lith. raũdas 'red'; OSlav. rudъ 'red,' ruda (Russ. rudá) 'ore' (originally 'ruddy'). But Skt. loha- 'reddish,' as noun 'copper, metal'; lohita- and rohita-, both 'ruddy'; rudhira- 'red,' as noun 'blood,' etc.

92. IE l = Skt. r or l

IE root lewk-, lowk- 'shine'; see above, §§ 80, 81. Note that all IE languages except Indo-Iranian show only l in this root, never r. But Skt. rocate 'shines' (IE lewketay); roca- 'shining' (IE lewke-); rocis- 'ray of light,' and many other forms with r. On the other hand, Skt. loka- 'world' (orig. 'light space'; IE lowko-); lokate and locate 'sees'; locana- 'illuminating'; as noun, 'eye'; and many other forms with l.

93. These examples are typical, and show clearly that in the same or related words, Skt. l and r both appear for IE r or l.

94. In the Rigveda, r is very much commoner; l is quite rare. In other words, the Rigveda is still fairly close to Indo-Iranian, which had only r for both. In later Skt., l increases in frequency, replacing Rigvedic r in some words, but it never becomes as common as r.

95. There are however some Middle Indic dialects which have only l, replacing r everywhere.

96. No law can be discerned by which Skt. chooses between r and l. Apparently it was a matter of dialect mixture. Some dialects changed Indo-Iranian r to l, either universally (as we just saw), or under conditions unknown to us. Sanskrit is a primarily r-dialect, which has borrowed from l-dialects rather extensively.

97. In any case, there is no correlation between either l or r of Skt. and either l or r of IE.

98. As stated above, IE r̥r and l̥l, the vocalic-consonantal allophones of the phonemes /r l/, appear in Sanskrit as ir or ur (or more rarely as il or ul, by the rule just stated). To put it otherwise, before IE consonantal r, l, IE vocalic r̥, l̥ became either i or u in Skt. No definite principle as to the choice between i and u has been discovered; but u prevails after labial consonants (p, ph, b, bh, m, v); otherwise i is usual.

99. The combinations r̥r, l̥l occurred, in IE times, only after a consonant and before a vowel, and only when the preceding consonant was itself preceded by another consonant or a long vowel (i. e. when the preceding syllable was prosodically long), or when the preceding consonant was initial in a speech utterance (§ 60, III). But in Skt. these conditions no longer hold fully; Skt. ir, ur (il, ul) from IE r̥r, l̥l, as well as the descendants of the parallel allophones of the other semivowels (IE iy, uw, m̥m, n̥n), sometimes occur when the preceding consonant is preceded by a short vowel; also in absolutely initial position, when there is no preceding consonant; and even before a consonant.

100. IE r̥r = Skt. ir (il), ur (ul)

IE g^wr̥reti ‘swallows’: Skt. girati and gilati ‘swallows’; cf. Gk. *βορός* ‘gobbling, greedy’; Lat. (carni-)vorus. When a short vowel precedes, IE g^wr- replaces g^wr̥r-: Skt. (Rigveda) (tuvi-)gra- ‘(mightily) swallowing.’

IE g^wr̥retay ‘lifts up the voice,’ esp. ‘praises,’ but also ‘cries out’: Skt. gurate ‘greets with joy’; related to Lat. grātus ‘welcome, pleasing’; and to Lith. gìrti ‘praise.’

101. IE l̥l = Skt. ir (il), ur (ul)

IE pl̥lo-, pl̥li- ‘stronghold’: Skt. pura-, puri- ‘stronghold’; Gk. *πόλις* ‘city’; Lith. pilìs ‘stronghold, castle.’

IE pl̥lu- ‘much’ (beside plu- after short vowel): Skt. puru- ‘much’; Gk. *πολύ(ς)*; Gth. filu (Ger. viel); somehow related is Lat. plūs.

102. IE vocalic m̥, n̥ both became Skt. a. Greek also has *α*. The other IE languages usually replace the vocalic nasal by a consonantal nasal preceded by a vowel, which varies from language to language: Lat. em, en (sometimes im, in); Germanic um, un; Lith. im, in; OSlav. ę (a nasalized e), which became Russian ja.

103. IE m̥ = Skt. a

IE k̑m̥tom ‘100’: Skt. çatam; Avestan satəm; Gk. (*ἑ-*)*κατόν*; Lat. centum; OIr. cét; Gth. hund; Lith šim̃tas; (OSlav. sъto, whence Russ. sto, irregular, thought by many to be a borrowed word. Expected would be OSlav. *sęto, Russ. *sjató; some think a form of this is contained in the final member of the Slav. word for ‘1000,’ OSlav. tysęšta, Russ. týsjacha, orig. ‘strong hundred.’).

104. IE n̥ = Skt. a

IE n̥- ‘not,’ negative prefix, in composition: Skt. a-(mr̥ta-, ‘immortal’); Gk. *ἄ(-μβροτος*, ‘immortal’); OLat. en-, Class. Lat. in-; Gth. OE. and general Gmc. un-. (Before vowels, Skt. and Gk. an- from IE n̥n-, originally only used after a word ending in a consonant preceded by another consonant or by a long vowel, but generalized by analogy of the numerous forms in a- plus consonant.)

105. IE vocalic-consonantal m̥m, n̥n appear, as we should expect, as am, an in Skt. and Gk. (cf. § 104). Their treatment in the other languages need not be discussed here: in Old Slavic they became ьm, ьn.

106. IE m = Skt. m

IE root men (mon) 'think.' IE menos- 'mind, thought': Skt. manas-; Gk. μένος. Many related words from the same root showing m-n: e.g. Lat. me-min-ī 'I remember'; Gth. (preterito-present) man 'I believe' (orig. 'have thought'); OE. man (same mg.).

107. IE n = Skt. n

IE root men (mon) 'think,' § 106.

Ablaut

108. We have not yet listed all the IE phonemes which, phonetically, functioned as vowels. Before naming the rest, it is desirable to discuss what is called IE *Ablaut.*

109. Ablaut means systematic correspondence between different vowels (or lack of them, 'zero vocalism'). It is sometimes called in English *vowel gradation.* Whenever different vowel phonemes appear in related words we may speak of Ablaut, as in English sing, sang, sung, song.

110. In Indo-European, we speak of *qualitative* and *quantitative* Ablaut.

111. Qualitative Ablaut is variation between vowels of different phonetic quality. In IE the varying vowels are usually e and o (also ē and ō); sometimes, but much more rarely, a and o (also ā and ō). (But never a and e.)

112. Quantitative Ablaut is variation between vowels which differ in quantity. In IE we find variation between e and ē, between o and ō, between a and ā, and between any of these vowels and zero (total loss of vowel).

113. Often, indeed typically, IE shows qualitative and quantitative Ablaut combined in one group of related words. That is, e. g., e varies with ē and with zero, but also with o or ō.

114. The typical primary scheme of IE ablaut shows three quantitative and two qualitative grades of vocalism. The quantitative are the *lengthened grade* or *Dehnstufe, normal* (or *full,* or *strong*) *grade,* and *zero grade* (or *weak grade*). The qualitative are called *e-grade* (in a few cases, *a-grade* instead) and *o-grade.* Thus, stem ped-, pod- 'foot':

Lengthened	ē ō	Lat. pēs (*pēds)	Doric Gk. πώς (*pōds)
Normal	e o	Lat. ped-is	Gk. ποδός
Zero	— (no vowel)	Avestan fra-bd-a 'forefoot' (-bd- for -pd-)	

115. Such variations were, in IE, not random. Originally they occurred each in prescribed situations or conditions. The normal e-grade was originally accented; its reduction to the zero grade accompanied, and was conditioned by, shift of the accent to another syllable. Many believe that the lengthened grade resulted from loss of an originally following syllable. The conditions of o-grade vocalism are much more obscure, and indeed still await any satisfactory explanation. But, to a considerable extent, each grade of Ablaut, qualitative as well as quantitative, seems to have occurred in IE in certain specific and typical situations.

116. For example, in present forms of what are called 'root-class' verbs, the singular active was regularly formed by adding the personal endings to the root in its normal e-grade, which was accented: IE és-ti 'he, she, it is': Skt. ásti; Gk. ἐστί (with shift of accent); Lat. est; OLith. esti. But the dual and plural were formed by adding the endings to the zero grade of the same root: IE s-énti (or s-ónti) 'they are': Skt. s-ánti; Lat. sunt.

117. Since we have seen that IE a, e, o all merged in Skt. a, and IE ā, ē, ō in Skt. ā, it is evident that IE *qualitative* Ablaut cannot remain in Skt. (At least not directly, in the quality of the vowels. We have seen, § 27, that it nevertheless has left an indirect trace; before Skt. a, ā from IE e, ē, the IE velars and labiovelars become Skt. palatals, just as before IE i, ī, y.) There is nothing in the Skt. vowels a, ā to show whether a comes from IE a, e, or o, and ā from IE ā, ē, or ō. We can therefore largely ignore IE qualitative Ablaut in Sanskrit.

118. *Ablaut of roots containing semivowels.* Often, in the normal grade, IE had a semivowel after the vowel. This semivowel, in this position, had to be consonantal, by the phonemic law determining pronunciation of IE semivowels, § 60, II (1) and (2). Less commonly, IE had a semivowel *before* the vowel; this had to be either consonantal, or vocalic plus consonantal, according to what preceded (§ 60, II (3) and III). In either case, the disappearance of the normal-grade vowel compelled the semivowel (before a consonant, or final) to assume vocalic function in the zero grade (§ 60, I). That is, to normal-grade *ey, oy, ay* or *ye, yo, ya* corresponded zero-grade *i*. And so, zero-grade *u* corresponded to normal-grade *ew* etc., *we* etc.; *r̥* to *er* etc., *re* etc., and so on. Thus we get schemes of quantitative Ablaut like the following, in which the normal grade shows a vowel plus consonantal semivowel (a diphthong), while the zero grade has only a vocalic semivowel. (Similar systems existed, less often, in which e, o, or a followed the semivowel in the normal grade.)—The lengthened grade in most roots was in IE much rarer than the other two. Secondary developments in Skt. made it much commoner there. In §§ 121-126 are quoted only a few cases of lengthened-grade forms which may with reasonable confidence be assumed to be IE inheritances; in many roots these are hard to find.

119. Indo-European:

Lengthened grade	ēy(ōy)	ēw(ōw)	ēr(ōr)	ēl(ōl)	ēm(ōm)	ēn(ōn)
Normal grade	ey(oy)	ew(ow)	er(or)	el(ol)	em(om)	en(on)
Zero grade	i	u	r̥	l̥	m̥	n̥

which in Sanskrit appear as:

Lengthened grade	āi	āu	ār(āl)	ār(āl)	ām	ān
Normal grade	e	o	ar(al)	ar(al)	am	an
Zero grade	i	u	ṛ	ṛ	a	a

120. In a complete statement, it would have to be added that before a following vowel (of a suffix, or of another word), the zero grade as stated above would be replaced by the consonantal, or (according to what precedes, § 60, III) the vocalic plus consonantal, form of the semivowel; that is, by

Indo-European	y(iy)	w(uw)	r(r̥r)	l(l̥l)	m(m̥m)	n(n̥n)
= Sanskrit	y(iy)	v(uv)	r or l (ir, ur, il, ul)		m(am)	n(an)

120a. The Hindu grammarians treated these same phenomena in their own fashion as the guṇa-vṛddhi system, tabulated in Whitney 236. They regarded our zero grade as basic and gave it no name. From it they derived the guṇa (our normal) grade by prefixing (Skt.) a (IE e, o, a), whereas we reverse this theory by starting with the normal or guṇa grade and assuming loss of the vowel in the zero grade. Our lengthened grade is the Hindu vṛddhi: they regarded it as formed by prefixing (Skt.) a to the normal grade (guṇa).

120b. The Skt. a-vowels do not really fit into the pattern set up by the Hindus. This is illustrated by the fact that they put a (and even ā) into both the guṇa and the (by them unnamed) zero grade. Actually, in original IE, the vowels a, e, o (= Skt. a) occurred only in the normal grade (Hindu guṇa), and ā, ē, ō (= Skt. ā) only in the lengthened grade (Hindu vṛddhi), except in 'heavy bases' (see § 127) where IE ā, ē, ō (Skt. ā) occurred in the normal grade. In the zero grade there was originally no vowel at all. Forms which show Skt. a in positions requiring zero grade vocalism are analogical, although some such analogical forms may have been created, secondarily, in late forms of IE itself.

Examples of Ablaut systems in roots containing semivowels

121. *Roots containing y*: IE ey (oy), i, 'go.'

Normal grade: IE ey-mi 'I go': Skt. é-mi; Gk. εἶ-μι; Lith. ei-mì 'I go.' Same grade in Slavic i-ti 'to go.'

Zero grade: IE i-te (or i-the) 'ye go': Skt. i-thá; Gk. ἴ-τε 'ye go.' Same grade in Lat. i-tiō 'going, motion.'

122. *Roots containing w*: IE k̑lew (k̑low), k̑lu, 'hear.'

Lengthened grade: IE k̑lēw-: Skt. aorist a-çrāu-ṣīt 'he heard.'

Normal grade: IE k̑lew-ter- 'one who hears': Skt. çro-tar-. IE k̑lew-os- 'fame': Skt. çravas-; Gk. κλέ(ϝ)ος. Same grade in OHG.hliu-(munt), Ger. Leumund 'reputation, report.'

Zero grade: IE k̑lu-to- 'heard': Skt. çru-ta- 'heard'; Gk. κλυτός 'famous'; Lat. in-clutus 'famous'; prior element in Germanic proper names like OHG.Hlud-(erīch), OE.Hloþ-(wīg) (Ger. Ludwig).

123. *Roots containing r*: IE bher (bhor), bhr̥ 'bear, carry.'

Lengthened grade: (o-grade) IE bhōr-: in Skt. bhāra- 'burden'; and in Gk. φώρ, φωρός 'thief'; φωριαμός 'chest for packing clothes.'

Normal grade: IE bher-ō 'I bear': Skt. bharā(mi); Gk. φέρω; Lat. ferō; Gth. baira, Eng. bear; OSlav. berą, Russ. bjerú 'I take.'

Zero grade: IE bhr̥-ti- 'carrying': Skt. bhṛti- 'carrying; maintenance, salary'; Lat. fors, abl. forte 'chance' (a 'bringing' of fate), fortūna; Gth. ga-baurþs 'birth,' Eng. birth, burden (older burthen).

124. *Roots containing l*: IE wel (wol), wl̥, 'will, wish, choose.'

Normal grade: IE welo- (wolo-) : Skt. vara- (probably IE welo-) 'choice, wish; (adj.) choice, excellent.' Same grade in Lat. volō (older velō); Gth. wiljan 'will' and (o-grade) waljan 'choose' (Ger. wählen); Lith. pa-vel-mi 'I will'; OSlav. vel-ją, Russ. vjeljú 'I command,' and (o-grade) OSlav. Russ. vólja '(free-)will.'

Zero grade: IE wl̥to- 'chosen, wished': Skt. vr̥ta-. Same grade in Lith. viltìs 'hope' ('wish'; IE wl̥tí-).

125. *Roots containing m*: IE g^wem (g^wom), g^wm̥, 'go, come.'

Normal grade: (o-grade) IE g^we-g^wom-a 'I went': Skt. jagama 'I went'; Gth. qam 'I came' (to infin. qiman 'to come' from IE g^wem-). (Eng. come and Ger. kommen are from zero-grade forms.)

Zero grade: IE g^wm̥ti- 'going, coming' (noun) : Skt. gati- 'going, gait, course'; Gk. βάσις 'step, tread, basis'; Lat. in-venti-ō 'coming at, invention'; Gth. ga-qumþs 'meeting.' From the same grade Gk. βαίνω 'go' and Lat. veniō 'come,' but there are difficulties and obscurities about both.

126. *Roots containing n*: IE men (mon), mn̥ 'think.'

Lengthened grade: IE mēn-: Vedic aorist (a-)māṅ-sta 'he thought.'

Normal grade: IE menos- 'thought': Skt. manas; Gk. μένος. From IE o-grade: Gk. μέ-μον-α, perfect, 'I think on'; cf. Lat. meminī 'I remember.'

Zero grade: IE mn̥-ti- 'act of thinking': Skt. mati-; Lat. mēns; Gth. ga-munds 'recollection,' OE. ge-mynd, Eng. mind; Lith. at-mintìs 'recollection'; OSlav. pa-mętь, Russ. pámjatj, 'recollection, memory.'

127. *Ablaut of 'Heavy Bases.'* In some IE roots, a long vowel (ā, ē, or ō) appears in positions which belong typically to the normal grade, not the lengthened grade; that is, in which most roots show short a, e, or o. Particularly striking are cases in which this long vowel is final in the root. For these are discordant with the phonetic pattern of IE in general. There is no IE root ending in short a, e, o; roots containing these vowels always end in a consonant (or semivowel, which in the normal grade must always be consonantal in function, § 60 above). But, in certain roots, IE long ē, ō, ā may end a root. Such roots are called *heavy bases*; the others, of the type we have previously talked about, are *light bases*. (Some heavy bases, however, show consonants after the long vowel of the normal grade, like light bases.)

128. The clearest evidence for a heavy base is occurrence of an IE long vowel in normal-grade situations, that is, where light bases show an IE short vowel (plus consonant or consonantal semivowel). Such a situation, for example, is that form of a root which precedes the IE noun-of-agent suffix -ter- (-tor-). Here the root shows normal grade. So Skt. bhar-tar- (IE bher-ter-, or -tor-) 'one who bears'; çro-tar- (IE k̑lew-ter-) 'one who hears,' etc. But Skt. dhā-tar- 'one who sets, establishes'; sthā-tar- 'one who stands'; dā-tar- 'one who gives,' which point to IE dhē-ter- or -tor-, sthā-tor- (Lat. stātor), dō-tor- (Gk. δώτωρ). These long vowels are not to be taken as lengthened grade forms; that grade does not appear before this suffix. The fact that these long vowels may be final in their roots, as in the examples cited, confirms our view that they are structurally something different from the IE ā, ē, ō which function as lengthened grades to IE a, e, o.

129. *Zero grade of heavy bases; IE ə 'shwa.'* What happens in the zero grade of these heavy bases? Is even a *long* IE normal-grade vowel lost in them?

130. There are a few forms which seem to look in that direction. But they are problematic, and probably to be explained otherwise.

131. The question should be answered by looking at forms which regularly show zero grade in light bases. Such a form is the past passive participle in IE -to- (or -no-), Skt. -ta- (-na-). Thus, from three light bases cited above, IE roots ey 'go,' k̑lew 'hear,' bher 'bear,' we have participles Skt. i-ta-, çru-ta-, bhr̥-ta- (IE i-to-, k̑lu-to-, bhr̥-to-), 'gone, heard, borne.'

132. The participles of the three heavy bases cited above are Skt. dhi-ta- (hi-ta-), sthi-ta-, and (in some compounds) -di-ta- (the usual datta- is secondary but easily explained).

133. Evidently Skt. i corresponds as zero grade to *normal grade* Skt. ā, whether this be derived from IE ā, ē, or ō.

134. This Skt. i cannot be derived from IE i, for two reasons. (1) No semivowel (y) appears in the normal grade forms of these roots. (2) In the IE languages outside of Indo-Iranian, even the zero grade contains no i, but rather (usually) the same vowel which otherwise represents IE a.

135. We must therefore posit a special IE zero-grade vowel, which it is customary to call *shwa* (a Hebrew term) and to write ə, as the IE zero-grade correspondent to normal-grade ā, ē, ō in heavy bases.

136. We then set up the phonetic law: IE ə becomes Skt. (and Iranian) i, but in other IE languages is treated like IE a.

This is confirmed by at least one word for which no normal-grade forms are known, but where the treatment is the same:

IE ə = Skt. i (Gk., Lat., Germ. a)

IE pəter- 'father': Skt. pitar-; Gk. πατήρ; Lat. pater; Gth. fadar, Eng. father.

137. IE ə was maintained, even in IE itself, only before consonants (including consonantal semivowels). It was always lost before vowels.

138. *Pre-Indo-European note.* According to many scholars of recent times, 'Indo-Hittite'—a common fore-runner of Indo-European and Hittite—contained four consonants called *laryngeals.* These, most of them believe, were lost in Indo-European, leaving lengthening of a preceding vowel when a consonant followed. Thus this school accounts for the normal-grade long vowels of IE heavy bases. IE ā, ē, ō in these heavy bases are derived from Indo-Hittite short vowels plus laryngeal consonants. Thus the heavy bases did not originally end in root-final vowels, but in laryngeal consonants; they fit better into the general IE pattern. See Sturtevant's *Indo-Hittite Laryngeals* (1942), 66 ff.

139. It has been suggested that IE ə may have been a correspondent of a laryngeal consonant, which assumed vocalic function when, in the zero grade, the normal-grade vowel disappeared, somewhat as the IE semivowels did in the same circumstances. Sturtevant's view, however, is different.

140. *Dissyllabic bases.* Not a few IE roots containing semivowels show, in their normal grade (before a consonant), dissyllabic forms, where the roots so far considered (both light and heavy) have monosyllabic forms.

141. The simplest and, for our purposes, most interesting of these dissyllabic forms are a group typefied by IE bhewə-, Skt. bhavi- 'become, come to be.' Here the first syllable has a normal e-grade vowel; a semivowel follows, and the second syllable contains IE ə, Skt. i. This and similar forms occur in situations where other roots have monosyllabic elements. So before the agent suffix IE -ter-, -tor-, Skt. bhavi-tar- 'one who becomes' contrasts with çro-tar- 'one who hears' (IE bhewə-tor-, k̂lew-tor-).

142. In the zero grade of such roots, for example in the past passive participle, we should theoretically expect (e. g.) an IE *bhwə-to-. Perhaps something like that may once have existed. Or, instead of *wə, perhaps it was once u plus a laryngeal consonant (see §§ 138-9). (We must in theory assume that ə is always a zero-grade to a heavy-base normal-grade ā, ē, or ō.)

143. But throughout the whole IE territory we find, instead of any such thing, either a long ū, or something which seems clearly to go back to an IE ū. The participle of the root IE bhewə was IE bhū-to-, Skt. bhū-ta-, 'become.' Similarly from a root IE neyə 'lead' we get a pple. IE nī-to-, Skt. nī-ta- 'led.' And while no r̥̄, l̥̄, m̥̄, n̥̄ is actually preserved as such in historic IE speech, there is good reason to believe that they existed in IE in cases analogous to such ī and ū. This assumption is based not only on the general parallelism between the six semivowels. It seems confirmed by some of the historic forms found in the zero grade of dissyllabic bases containing r, l, m, n; they seem in various ways to recommend the assumption of long vocalic semivowels.

144. A set of parallel forms will help to make clear these conditions. In each pair of roots, the first is monosyllabic, the second dissyllabic. For each root we cite the reconstructed IE, and the actual Sanskrit, noun of agent in IE -ter- or -tor- (Skt. -tar-), with normal grade of root, and the past passive participle in IE -to- or -no- (Skt. -ta- or -na-), with zero grade. (Page 29.)

145. We therefore set up six long vowels peculiar to the zero-grade of dissyllabic bases containing semivowels, which phonetically seem to have been lengthenings of the six vocalic forms of the semivowels: ī, ū, r̥̄, l̥̄, m̥̄, n̥̄. These were not, in IE, members of

IE root	Normal grade IE	Normal grade Skt.	Zero grade IE	Zero grade Skt.
ey (oy) : i 'go'	ey-tor-	e-tar- 'one who goes'	i-to-	i-ta- 'gone'
neyə (noyə) : nī 'lead'	neyə-tor-	nayi-tar-	nī-to-	nī-ta-
k̂lew (k̂low) : k̂lu 'hear'	k̂lew-tor-	çro-tar-	k̂lu-to-	çru-ta-
bhewə (bhowə) : bhū 'become'	bhewə-tor-	bhavi-tar-	bhū-to-	bhū-ta-
bher (bhor) : bhr̥ 'bear'	bher-tor-	bhar-tar-	bhr̥-to-	bhṛ-ta-
terə (torə) : tr̥̄ 'traverse'	terə-tor-	tari-tar-	tr̥̄-no-	tīr-ṇa-
ĝhwel (ĝhwol) : ĝhwl̥ 'be crooked'	ĝhwel-tor-	hvar-tar- [4]	ĝhwl̥-to-	hvṛ-ta-
pelə (polə) : pl̥̄ 'fill'	pelə-tor-	pari-tar- [4]	pl̥̄-no-	pūr-ṇa-
men (mon) : mn̥ 'think'	men-tor- [5]	man-tar-	mn̥-to-	ma-ta-
ĝenə (ĝonə) : ĝn̥̄ 'beget'	ĝenə-tor- [5]	jani-tar-	ĝn̥̄-to-	jā-ta-

[4] These forms are cited from Hindu grammarians; other normal-grade forms from the same roots confirm them.

[5] Cf. Latin mentor, genitor.

the semivowel phonemes, altho they were derived historically from combinations of the semivowels with some other sounds (either IE ə or its ancestor, or a laryngeal consonant).

146. In some cases, such as IE mūs 'mouse' (below), we find such vowels in isolated words, showing no clear relations with other words. These are presumed to be remnants of otherwise lost Ablaut systems.

The Sanskrit resultants of these sounds were as follows:

147. IE ī = Skt. ī

IE g^{w}īwo- 'living, alive, lively': Skt. jīva- 'alive'; Lat. vīvus; Lith. gývas; OSlav. zhivъ, Russ. zhiv. Related, but seemingly derived from a form with short i: Gk. βίος 'life'; Gth. qius 'living'; with a suffix derived from IE -g-, OE. cwicu, Eng. quick.

148. IE ū = Skt. ū

IE mūs- 'mouse': Skt. mūs-; Gk. μῦς; Lat. mūs; OE. OHG. (etc.) mūs; OSlav. myšь, Russ. mysh.

149. IE r̥̄ = Skt. īr, ūr

Cf. Skt. ir, ur, from IE r̥r and l̥l. Instead of īr, ūr, we might expect to find sometimes īl, ūl, but no such case has been noted for either IE r̥̄ or l̥̄. After labial consonants, ūr is usual, otherwise īr; but there are exceptions.

IE r̥̄mo- 'arm': Skt. īrma- 'arm, fore-leg of an animal'; Lat. armus; Gth. arms, Eng. arm; OSlav. ramo 'shoulder' (Russ. antiquated and literary, plural only, ramjená 'shoulders').

150. IE l̥̄ = Skt. īr, ūr

See note under IE r̥̄, which applies here also.

IE root (zero grade) ml̥̄dh- 'top' or the like: Skt. mūrdh-an- 'head, top'; Gk. βλωθ-ρός, 'tall,' for *μ(β)λ-, cf. ἄ-μ(β)ροτος 'immortal'; OE. molda 'top of the head.'

151. IE m̥̄ = Skt. ā

IE ĝm̥̄-ro-: Skt. jā-ra-, 'suitor, lover'; related to Gk. γαμβρός 'son-in-law' and to the root of Gk. γαμέω 'marry.' (A related form in lengthened grade: Skt. jām-ātar- 'son-in-law.') Probably from IE ĝm̥̄- with a different suffix: OSlav. zętь, Russ. zjatj 'son-in-law.'

Note: the Skt. participles of dissyllabic roots containing m are all formed like IE demə-, Skt. dami-(tar-) 'subdue,' past pple. Skt.

dānta- ‘subdued.’ This is best regarded as for original *dā-ta- (IE dm̥̄-to-) with nasal (originally m, assimilated to n before t) analogically inserted under the influence of normal and lengthened grade forms.

152. IE n̥̄ = Skt. ā

IE ĝn̥-to- ‘born’ (pple. to ĝenə-): Skt. jāta- ‘born’; Lat. (g)nātus (cf. co-gnātus); Gth. (himina-)kunds ‘heaven-born,’ OE. (heofon-)cund.

Note: an intrusive nasal is very much rarer in the participles of dissyllabic roots containing n than in those with m; but it occurs in Skt. pple. dhvānta- ‘sounded’ (normal grade dhvani- ‘sound’).

153. *Table of Sanskrit Vowels with their possible IE originals.*

Skt. a from	IE a, e, o, m̥, n̥
ā	ā, ē, ō, m̥̄, n̥̄
i	i, ə (and Skt. ir, il from r̥r, l̥l)
ī	ī (and Skt. īr from r̥̄, l̥̄)
u	u (and Skt. ur, ul from r̥r, l̥l)
ū	ū (and Skt. ūr from r̥̄, l̥̄)
ṛ	r̥, l̥
ḷ	(only Skt. root kḷp; perhaps IE r̥)
ṝ	See [6]
(ḹ does not occur)	
e	ay, ey, oy
āi	āy, ēy, ōy
o	aw, ew, ow
āu	āw, ēw, ōw

[6] Skt. ṝ occurs only in the acc. pl. and gen. pl., and nom.-acc. pl. neuter, endings of noun-stems in -r-, e. g. dātṝn, dātṝṇām. It has no prehistory, since these endings are late analogical creations, in imitation of the corresponding cases of i and u stem nouns. The analogical proportion would be:

agni-bhis : agnīn : agnīnām =
çatru-bhis : çatrūn : çatrūṇām =
dātṛ-bhis : dātṝn : dātṝṇām.

www.ingramcontent.com/pod-product-compliance
Lightning Source LLC
Chambersburg PA
CBHW051051030426
42339CB00006B/298
* 9 7 8 1 7 2 5 2 8 1 0 5 9 *